"Physician Heal Thyself"

Linda,

Enjoy your own journeys.
Live life in the precious
present!

Love

[signature]

"Physician Heal Thyself"

A Doctor's Spiritual Journey to the Holy Lands

Scott L Wiesen MD

ISBN: 1540849961
ISBN 13: 9781540849960

FOREWORD

THIS BOOK HAS been a labor of love from the outset. This entire journey was inspired by forces much greater than myself. I would like to thank my wife and children for their unwavering support throughout the entire process. There are many people who helped contribute to the final product, but I would especially like to thank Mel Ernst for her patience and willingness to convert my words into a published manuscript. I would also like to thank Mike Lusk, Barbara Walker, Sherry Scaccia, Joe Spano, and Gary Stewart for their invaluable editing assistance. Mostly, however, I would like to thank God for the opportunity to have these life changing adventures and all the blessings I have had and continue to have in this incarnation.

LOVE

Day 1: The Journey

THE JOURNEY IS often as meaningful as the destination, yet it seems as though we are always in a hurry? As an old salty dog sailor, I learned through many trials and tribulations to try and enjoy every moment of the present. The "precious present" is just that. Sadly so many of us are looking forward to tomorrow or feeling bad about yesterday and skipping today. Life in the precious present teaches us to enjoy it all.

This is one of the most important lessons in life. Most of us never realize that the most beautiful gift we have is the here and now. The PRECIOUS PRESENT. I was given a children's book in my 30's by this title that affects me to this day. Even in life's most difficult times, if we can learn to enjoy the here and now we will be so far ahead of the game. It is absolutely important to remember the past and unavoidable to look forward to the future, but if we forget the present we lose sight of the most important moment ever... NOW! Live life to its fullest extent. We all have good times and bad times. The precious present, however is the absolute time to live your life.

The genesis of my journey was circumstantial as is all of life. A good friend was contemplating a "walkabout". He was ready to escape for six to twelve months to find himself and explore the world. He was thinking of starting in Tibet. Now at this point in my life I had already been blessed to have traveled to many parts of the globe on numerous occasions. I often picked up charter sailboats all over the world as a fascinating way to see Italy, Spain, France, Greece, The South Pacific, The Bahamas, The Caribbean, Thailand, Australia, New Zealand and many other beautiful destinations. Nevertheless, Tibet was at the top of my proverbial bucket list. As I pondered this adventure the next day, I realized that due to a recent physical aliment, climbing in Tibet made this trip potentially hazardous at this time in my life. In a sudden moment of clarity, I realized I must visit the other spot on the top of my bucket list, the Holy Land immediately or I may be unable to travel there also. I had to grab the bull by the horn and just do it! As Yoda says, "Do or Do Not, there is no Try"

Thankfully, my wife has always been incredibly understanding when it came to my wanderlust. She thought it was dangerous for us both to go because of our children but she supported my adventure wholeheartedly. There clearly is great wisdom in the statement "behind every good man is an even better woman". I bought a ticket to Israel the next day with no itinerary in mind. I just knew I had to go.

As a child, I slept with a homemade pyramid made out of cardboard and tinfoil carefully aligned to the magnetic parts of the compass above my bed. I knew I also had to somehow get to Egypt as part of this journey and through some research, found the safest way to get there was through Jordan. I now had a plan. One of my favorite sayings that I always live by is, "You have to have a plan. If you don't have a plan you can't change it." In other words spontaneity is wonderful and essential to any great adventure. Go with the flow! That's always where many of life's most amazing opportunities and experiences arise. Nevertheless, complete spontaneity in my experience often leads to chaos and confusion. Don't be afraid to make a plan and be organized. Just be willing to change it when a better opportunity arises. Trust in the force. Learn to be lucky. All my life I have been told by many people how lucky I am. To quote the great Louis Pasteur, "Luck favors the prepared mind". Be prepared to be lucky.

I have been a seeker of the truth for years. I was raised Jewish and surrounded by Christians my whole life. During my quest, I have also studied Buddhism, read the old and new testament, sought out other seekers for their knowledge, including Atheists, Agnostics, American Indians, Christians, Jews, Hindu's, Buddhists and Muslims. When I was young I even perused Carlos Castaneda and the teachings of Don Juan. Unfortunately at the time that was like giving gun powder to a child. Nevertheless, my quest continues to this day.

Like many of us, spirituality and my desire to find Gods truth and love was indeed a QUEST as it still is to this day. This particular journey came about at the perfect time in my life. I was ready to open up my souls portals and see what might seep in. I was prepared to make my spiritual journey to the Holy Lands… the heart of the world.

LOVE

DAY 2

UPON ARRIVAL IN Tel Aviv, after an appropriately long arduous journey, I never felt so alive in my life. I checked into my hotel in Tel Aviv. After a shower and a short nap I went down to the pool for lunch. As is usually the case in life, some of the most important lessons happen when you least suspect them. Most of life's great adventures include temptation. I was venturing on a spiritual journey so women and lust were the farthest things from my mind. There is an old Jewish saying however, "man plans, and God laughs." EXACTLY!

When I got to the pool, I soon realized it was not an ordinary Saturday. One bachelorette party would have been decadent enough, (but you can't make this stuff up), there were three separate bachelorette parties going on around the pool this day! I realized immediately the irony because there were THREE, the magic number that comes up so often in my life. The overabundance and decadence of the situation literally made me laugh out loud. Whilst I harbor absolutely no suspicions that I am a great master in this incarnation, all the great masters had temptation early on as part of their spiritual journey. The force went out of the way to make this one so obvious and over the top, it was very easy to avoid. Nevertheless, I truly appreciated the irony of the event.

That evening, I contemplated walking a mile up the beach to visit Jaffa, the old port city on the Mediterranean. (See figures 1 and 2) I was told at the hotel that it was perfectly safe to walk there. It was Friday night, which is the Sabbath or the beginning of the holy 24 hour period for the Jews. As it turns out, the Arab population of Tel Aviv takes over the beach on Friday nights for barbeques and family fun. Now remember, all we hear on our news reports is the dangers of the Middle East. I was actually frightened to walk amongst all these Arabs as an American Jew. Meanwhile, they were all having delicious food and family entertainment along the beach while I was being the brainwashed scared American. The Arabs and the Jews live together in harmony in Tel Aviv. The real problems are with the non-Israeli Palestinians living in the West Bank and Gaza Strip. It rapidly became clear that this was a very precarious situation with no obvious solutions. No one, including myself, truly understands why we have this distrust and fear.... but it is pervasive. Hence, the Arabs and the Jews have been at war for thousands of years. "Things that make you go Hmmm..."

The longer we live in this world, the more we realize there are no accidents. Subsequently, even the bad times offer us the opportunity to have learning experiences. In fact, I believe there are even greater opportunities to learn through life's more difficult experiences (I know....drag). We just have to learn to embrace them. The good times are the rewards. The bad times are school time... The time to learn some of the most important lessons. PAY ATTENTION! The precious present is just that. The here and now is the most precious gift one has. Enjoy every moment of it. Try to remember on the difficult days, that that's when the real learning is going on. If you pass the tests (and no one fails for real, sometimes you just have to keep retaking the test until we get it right), then we get the rewards.

LESSON 1: THE LAW OF KARMA

If you learn or remember anything from this story, I encourage you to acknowledge karma. Karma is the one absolute rule of the universe. That and love is the answer to every question. Wikipedia stated it refers to "The spiritual principal of cause and effect where intent and actions of an individual influence the future of that individual".

Simply stated, God knows your heart. He knows your intent and reasons for all your actions. Positive behavior and intent lead to "good Karma" and subsequent rewards. Sadly, the inverse is also true. As a parent, I must say this one has always been the hardest to teach, but always the one absolute rule of the universe and therefore very important to pass on. The rest is often just window dressing. While the universal force, God if you will, is aware of everything, man still has free will. The force happily lets man continue on his journey making choices constantly, with one rule governing all our behavior. The law of Karma. There are no accidents. There is no reason to necessarily ascribe traits such as good and bad to Karma....that is for God and God alone. But it is Gods universal rule of cause and effect.

There is no escaping karma. Whatever your religious beliefs, whatever your cultural upbringing, it is an essential lesson of this crazy little thing called life. Every decision we make in life is fraught with a positive and negative effect. If ones heart is pure and your intentions are pure, then karma is in your favor and your life will usually be blessed. Sadly, the inverse is also true. If we fill our hearts with love, and let that affect are actions, the world will open up and your life will become bountiful and blessed. Try it... Please. God loves all his children. Subsequently, he doesn't mind if you make mistakes. Nevertheless, the law of karma governs all of us and all our actions. Even God with all his love, has no problem continuously enforcing his one absolute rule. Therefore, fill your heart with love and use the force to guide all your decisions.

LOVE

DAY 3

I AWOKE AND met my guide and driver in my hotel in Tel Aviv. We were traveling to Galilee by way of Caesareum and Acre. As my guide educated me about the Roman rule of the Middle East, the Crusades, and the Sunni/Shiite battles, it struck me as truly ironic that most wars in the history of mankind have used Gods name as a rationalization and an inspiration to BOTH sides? Both sides believe they are carrying Gods banner to victory. The irony is sadly catastrophic, although it is certainly not my job to judge other people's behaviors. Nevertheless, this one is very hard. I truly love all man, but sadly to this day, many want to kill me for my religious convictions or even my parent's beliefs. Hitler killed anyone who was even one quarter Jewish (one grandparent), so I found it quite beautiful that the rules to immigrate into Israel were similar. If you could be killed for being 25% Jewish, you could immigrate into Israel with the same background. I was surprised at the amount of Ukrainian/Russian immigrants in Israel until I learned of this rule.

Once again though, "Judge not lest ye be judged". Nevertheless, it is being done all over the world. We are constantly judging one another. Catholics and Protestants murdering each other in Northern Ireland. Why? Are they praying to a different master? Were there 2 different masters named Jesus? Even today, we see intense prejudice based on what? Craziness! Christians killing the Jews and Muslims during the Crusades, Christians murdering Jews during the Spanish inquisition and once again during Hitler's reign just to name a few of the atrocities in the history of mankind. Now in America we are shocked to learn that Sunnis and Shiites are killing each other because they are the wrong type of Muslim? It is all insanity! As I thought of all this,

I was very emotionally torn. I was raised Jewish, but I have become a nondenominational lover of God and seeker of the truth and love.

Once I was finally settled in that evening overlooking the Sea of Galilee, I was filled with amazing energy. Perhaps it was checking into the Scotts (my name) Hotel and being put into the doctor's suite that I began to know this was no ordinary adventure. As I relaxed and began my meditation and prayers, I asked the master Jesus to show me his presence and I felt it immediately. I was overwhelmed with pure joy and felt the full force of God's love. As I looked over towards Syria across the Golan Heights, across the Sea of Galilee, (See figure 3) I asked God to shine his light and help these people understand his true message. Don't kill people in God's name. I may not know much, but I know he doesn't want that!

As I went to bed that evening, I knew this was a very special place and great things awaited me. This was going to be a very special journey.
LOVE

DAY 4

THIS DAY TURNED out to be one of the most incredible days of my life. Understanding the concept of the precious present means every day is special. Most importantly, every day has the opportunity to be the best day of one's life. Nevertheless, my day in Galilee exceeded my expectations which were very high. It started on an antique boat in the Sea of Galilee meant to resemble an old fishing vessel from the time of Christ. Traversing the waters where Jesus preached I was struck with a feeling of pure love. (See figure 4) As my guide so aptly explained, in Israel everything pertaining to size is overstated in the Bible. The Jordan River is actually a creek and the Sea of Galilee is a small lake. Indeed....but the energy and power was immense!

Growing up as a sailor, the water has always been my friend and my first home. The energy was breathtaking. My guide pointed out Capernaum, which was Peter's home on the lake. We also saw the Mount of Beatitudes where Jesus gave his sermon. (See figure 5) I was not scheduled to go to either place originally, likely because of my Jewish surname; I rapidly rectified this and arranged a visit to both after our cruise.

On arrival in Capernaum, I knew this was indeed a very special place. (See figure 6) Walking the earth in Jesus's footsteps was as powerful as one might imagine. Over Peters' home, a glass bottomed structure was built so people could sit comfortably and pray while observing Christ's disciples home and very likely where Jesus himself slept. (See figures 7 and 8)

Throughout Israel, at many historic sites, there is often more than one area marking religious sites depending on which denomination is in charge. In Capernaum this was not the case. There was only one home of Peter in this beautiful lakeside village. For whatever reason, I found great peace and love here. The building was full of 50-60 seekers at most times as it was that day. As I meditated, I found myself floating across the sea filled with pure joy. It was then that Jesus came to me and held my hand as we floated above the Sea of Galilee. There was pure love. A true treasured moment in the space time continuum and one that I will never forget. After some indeterminate time passed, I was filled with the master's pure energy and my body was vibrating at a very high level. Strangely, as I came back to reality and opened my eyes, the church was completely empty? All the other seekers were gone. There are no accidents.

Ironically, as an aside, at our next stop in Tzfat, I realized my phone must have fallen out of my pocket during my meditation as it was gone. As this was my camera for the trip, it was a possession I wanted. My guide apologized and said we would never get it. My driver concurred. They stated that even in Israel and the Holy Lands, people are still people. Interestingly, I KNEW it wasn't gone. I visualized it. He called there on my behalf and warned me in advance again that it would likely not be found. I just smiled. When he got off the phone, he had a look of bewilderment. He said not only was it found, but it was with a guide friend of theirs who was going to drop it off at the Kibbutz they were staying. I was not surprised as I KNEW. My guide and driver just laughed and said I was "incredibly lucky". I was very appreciative and grateful for all the wonders of the cosmic.

As we were driving to Tzfat, my guide stated this was the historical home of the Kabbalah (the heart of Jewish mystical studies). He knew of my interest in mysticism and thought I would find it fascinating. After the debacle with my phone and a brief lunch, we stopped in a few synagogues but everyone was out for lunch. As it turns out, Tzfat is also one of the main artist galleries in Israel. As a musician who has supported the Arts for years, I found it fascinating the close connection between mysticism and the arts. Again, there are no accidents. As we wandered through a few galleries we ended up in one

SCOTT L WIESEN MD

looking at a map of Israel made out of the shape of a dove. I didn't know at the time that this dove would become my spirit guide, but like all great adventures, they must start somewhere. As I was admiring this piece, the owner of the gallery introduced himself. I was wearing jeans and a simple shirt at the time that the owner asked me in the midst of the conversation, "Are you a physician?" The question surprised me as it was out of context, but I said, "Yes I was". He then showed me another picture of the Physician's prayer from the Kabbalah. It was very beautiful. As we started talking, his wife the artist entered the gallery and it was her birthday. We all talked for some time as we formed a connection and I purchased the paintings (both pieces now hang in my home and office).

At some point in the conversation, the owner of the gallery asked me if I wanted to come see his home as it was quite special and he thought I would find it very interesting. I was somewhat surprised, but I privately asked my guide if it was safe to venture there. He said he has known the gallery owner for years and he has never been invited to his home, but it was certainly safe. Off we went.

As we were walking to his home, he explained to me that he was the seventeenth generation in this home. He also told me I was going to like this adventure more than the pyramids (Really?). I thought that was quite an ostentatious statement at the time...but...perhaps, in retrospect, he was correct. A quick math problem let me know we were talking about a very old home if he was the 17th generation in the dwelling. As we entered and looked around, it was very beautiful. His wife was an artist, so as you can imagine it was decorated magnificently with art hanging everywhere and very tasteful furniture. There were stunning vistas to Lebanon to the North and the Golan Heights and Syria to the East. It was then that we started to go down into the antechambers of the home. After descending many levels we finally arrived.

It was a very old room filled with incredible power. I stopped and literally fell to my knees! I was overcome with an incredible feeling of Deja Vu. It was overwhelming. As I looked over, the shop owner had a giant smile on his face and was actually giggling. He just said, "I told you so." He then stated, "Do you think it was an accident I asked if you were a doctor?" He knew who I was.

As it turns out, this room had many tunnels and hiding spots and escape routes as it turned out to be one of the original places where the Kabbalah was inspired, written, and studied by his ancestors and their friends. Had I been there before? Sometimes words can only act like a painting of a sunset. The natural beauty is beyond reproach. What an incredible experience.

As I gathered my wits, and headed off to the Mount of Beatitudes down the way, I recollected the amazing adventures I had already experienced this incredible day. As we arrived at the place of the Sermon on the Mount, I sought out a bible to read the Beatitudes. There were none available that I could find in English. A lovely nun found a small pocket bible in English which she gave to me. I was a 54 year old man at the time with eyes made to read ordinary size books with the assistance of reading glasses. This book was a miniature pocket Bible and I had no glasses. As I searched and found a secluded spot for my meditation and reading of the Beatitudes, the full power of Jesus and his love came to me. I read the entirety of the Beatitudes from this miniature Bible with my eyes functioning temporarily like a 30 year old man again? I wept openly in wonder when I was done. I was filled with love and gratitude.

As the day ended and I recounted my adventures, I called my nurse at home who is also a seeker. She was amazed as she was just reading the Beatitudes at the time of my phone call. Her bible was still open to those pages. I told her, "of course it was"… synchronicity. All I could think of as I retired for the day was to allow the golden rule (do unto others as you would have others do unto you) and love to continue to guide my path. I wrote in my journal then, "I shall continue my journey with my eyes and my heart wide open".

LOVE

DAY 5

I AWOKE TO a beautiful morning in Galilee refreshed and full of vitality. As I spoke to my lovely bride that morning, she told me after hearing of my adventures the day before that perhaps my ultimate quest on this journey was not the pyramids but something else? I did not concur, but I have always trusted her instincts. Nevertheless, she was raised as a quite fundamental Baptist so she was all for Jesus entering my life. However, I still knew there was much more to this journey and anxiously awaited my next adventure.

Our first stop was in Al Nasra. The Christians say this was Nazareth, as in Jesus the Nazarene. I found this interesting as it was 60km away from the Sea of Galilee where Jesus preached. Why would Jesus live so far from where he preached? This reminded me of a book by H Spencer Lewis entitled "The Mystical Life of Jesus" which never questioned the Christ and his place in the world, just some of the historical account for those that may be interested.

As I was having my morning meditation in a lovely church built around a grotto, where Mary purportedly lived, I awoke and stared upon a beautiful alter. It was there that I saw a pyramid above a picture of Jesus with a 3rd eye in the middle of the pyramid. (See figures 9 and 10) Once again, I felt the full power of God's presence and I knew the image was for me and my wife. I took a photo and sent it to her. Little did I know at the time, but my white dove was also right there in the picture. Another wonderful gift.

Edit

After visiting more ancient ruins and trekking thru the length of the west bank, we stopped along the River Jordan just past Jericho. As my son is named Joshua, who fought the battle of Jericho, it seemed to be very special to me. The site was one of many purported to be the site of John the Baptist's meeting with Jesus along the river Jordan (my other son's name) and baptizing him in God's name. (My poor daughter Rachel had no landmarks named after her, but then again her name, Rachel Elizabeth, came to me in a dream while I was in college).

As I stopped and prayed, I asked John the Baptist to come baptize me. (See figure 11) Once again, the spirit of God or the Holy Ghost or whatever you choose to call it, came upon me and the spirit of the lord helped me cleanse my spirit and repent in the river Jordan. "Ask and it will be given to you; seek and you will find; knock and the door will be opened to you". (Mathew 7:7)

As we left the west bank we journeyed into the heart of the world, Jerusalem. I thought my day was over but as the epicenter of Judaism, Islam and Christianity... Jerusalem turned out to be full of surprises. I was staying in the King David hotel just outside the walls of the old city; I was eating dinner at a fabulous restaurant just across the street from one of the walled gates. My guide was not with me but I felt compelled to visit the western wall. I knew it was crazy as it was dusk and I had no idea where I was going. I asked the waitress if it were safe and she said, "You're a big guy, you will probably be fine." Not exactly a ringing endorsement, but off I went. Remember, if you don't have a plan, you can't change it.

It was actually a walk of trepidation, as I had no idea where I was going and most of the shops were closed or closing. The streets were full of Palestinian merchants. As a Jew, I was truly frightened. I almost turned around on more than one occasion. Nevertheless, I ventured the rest of the way memorizing my path. When I first saw the western wall I teared up immediately? When I touched the wall I cried like a baby? The power was breathtaking. There were many people praying that evening. I closed my eyes and went into a deep mediation. When I awoke and looked up, I saw a white dove just above my head sitting inside the wall looking at me. I knew this dove was for me. (See figures 12 and 13) He was part of my vision quest, my spirit guide. I had dreamt before the trip I would find one just as an old high school friend who was an American Indian did when he set out on his journey. I had been fascinated with this concept ever since. It is strange what we remember at different times. Regardless, I knew the dove was a gift, just as the picture I purchased the day before was of a dove. I felt an oneness with the dove, and it helped complete me in some strange way. God is great and works in many mysterious ways. Open your eyes and your hearts.

LOVE

DAY 6

THE MORNING IN Jerusalem started in the garden of Gethsemane. I began to realize there were often multiple sites controlled by different religions claiming to be the original source. Does it really matter? Many paths to the same truth. Whatever gets you to the truth is just fine with the source.

The garden is essentially an olive grove outside the walls of the city. There were many of them all around. I climbed across a barrier and had a wonderful meditation in the garden feeling the full power of the heart of the world, Jerusalem. (See figure 12) This truth is at least partially geographically based. The known world was much smaller then. Israel ran along the sea surrounded by desert. One could only imagine that all travelers going north and south from Europe, Africa, and Asia

traversed through this essential land bridge. I doubt it was an accident that three of the world's largest religions (Buddhism hates to be called a religion...just a philosophy of life); Judaism, Christianity, and Islam all claim it to be their home.

Walking thru Jerusalem was breathtaking. I suspect anyone would feel all the power and love of the old city if they dared to open his or her heart. (See figure 13) I arrived again at the western wall. There were no doves, as I checked, because I thought maybe they just always stayed there....but no. During a beautiful meditation, I cried again while touching the wall. It was then, at least to me, I understood why it was called the "Wailing Wall". I was told God despised all the murder, violence, and evil done while carrying the God flag done by ALL religions. In America, we are shocked by the atrocities in the Arab world, but we conveniently forget the crusades where Christians slaughtered thousands of Muslims and Jews, again carrying the God flag. I remember, to this day, walking thru the Vatican and seeing tapestries glorifying the crusades with soldiers literally carrying a flag with a cross on it and felt nothing but pure evil. More recently, Hitler's atrocities are swept under the rug and even denied by many as Jewish nonsense. It is very sad. Nevertheless, the place has been imbued with an incredible energy which should and could be felt by everyone paying attention.

My guide then took me along the final walk of Christ as it was written. All the historical spots were marked with Roman numerals ironically. When I was in line where Christ was purportedly nailed to the cross, the Holy Spirit came to me, but it was also a place of sadness for me? When I laid my hand on the bedrock where his cross sat, (see figures 14 and 15) I strangely felt the need to apologize to God for man's behavior. Although, it was certainly not my place, I felt saddened but obligated to do so. At least historically, Jesus was preordained to die for our sins, and therefore was only fulfilling prophesy. Nevertheless, it came to me then that I felt certain if another great messenger of God came tomorrow, man would likely attempt to kill him again. The fear of man. The fear of the unknown. The fear of change. Finally, of course, the fear of losing power. Jesus was correct. "No one can serve two masters. For you will hate one and love the other, you will be devoted to one and despise the other. You cannot serve both God and money". (Mathew 6:24) If you love God and follow the golden rule, the rest will take care of itself.

After leaving the church, while searching for a cross for my wife, my instincts and God's guidance (one in the same), did not let me down. My spiritual path has included the study of the words of the Rosicrucian (the Rose Cross) American founder H Spencer Lewis for almost 14 years now (crcsite.org). I wanted to find a cross with a rose in the middle. My guide who has been there for years said, "I would never find a rose cross. I have never seen one." I passed an Arab store and felt the need to go in but my guide said it was not the safest and I would be better off elsewhere. After looking through a few stores he took me to, I made him take me back to the place he wasn't comfortable with. Of course I immediately found my rose cross with rose petals in the middle of a Jerusalem cross. The other 4 sides had Jerusalem stones, earth, and olive oil filling the glass portals. In front of my guide, I asked the Arab shop keeper to repeat what was in the middle of the cross. He said it was a rose. I smiled and was again called "extremely lucky" (ok… all my life I have been told this). Interestingly as an aside, the cross now sits in my home. In transit, the olive oil drained out of the bottom glass and it only contained air. A few days after I came home I realized the cross contained the four elements (air, water {olive oil}, earth {the Jerusalem stone}, and fire {the red rose petals}). I say a prayer every morning with my rose cross. It is very special to me.

Sadly, as we walked away from the Arab market, a merchant was shouting in Arabic, "Kill all the Jews"… Hence, The Wailing Wall!

That evening after dinner, I went back to the Western Wall to pray. This time with no trepidation. Once again, I had a lovely meditation and felt all the power and glory of God. I realized if I lived there, I would likely go most nights to pray there as so many Jerusalem citizens do. An amazing energy spot. When my meditation was over and I was walking away, I heard something or felt a presence. I didn't understand what it was but I felt compelled to turn around and go back. As I looked up, my white dove was back and he was talking to me. (See figures 16 and 17) He couldn't believe I wouldn't acknowledge him while I was praying there? Again, I dropped to my knees in awe and wonder and knew without any doubt that my white dove was my spirit guide forever. It was one of the most powerful, beautiful moments of my life (until he kept coming back throughout my journey). I was again moved to tears (I know…what a cry baby), but clearly a defining moment in my life.

LOVE

DAY 7

SADLY BUT VERY importantly the day started at the Holocaust memorial. More killing done in God's name. Although this has happened continuously throughout eternity, NEVER FORGET! It can and likely will happen again. It is happening today among the Arabs with the Sunni and Shiites killing each other despite praying to the same master and the same God. It is very sad. It not only likely will continue to happen, but it can occur way more easily than people will ever realize.

My first exposure to the New Testament was in a Great Books class in 11th grade. Our assignment was reading the first gospel Mathew. After experiencing the beautiful inspirational words of Jesus, my views toward organized religion were changed dramatically forever. It was hard to comprehend that I was never exposed to the words of such a divine master despite many years of religious studies? This troubled me greatly and made me question for the first time the motivations of some of the evangelical hierarchy of all religions. My second experience with the modern bible was when my wife asked me to read the New Testament as a birthday present to her a few years ago. I loved the first three synoptic gospels and was deeply moved. The words, written in red, Christ's words, were once again very beautiful and inspirational. Sadly, however, with multiple uses of the phrase, "The Jews" in the book of John with more than half used in a negative fashion (whilst there are no mentions of "The Jews" in the synoptic gospels used in a negative fashion), I felt many verses in the book of John helped foster the antisemitism that exists in the world today and this troubled me especially growing up Jewish and witnessing prejudice all my life. Most Christians won't pick up on the anti-Semitic statements as they read through the book of John as they didn't grow up Jewish surrounded by all the prejudice. My wife and her family still don't understand. I only knew what I felt when I read it. With numerous uses of "The Jews" used in a negative polemical fashion, the impression conveyed is one of hostility and non-acceptance towards Jews. I encourage true seekers to investigate antisemitism in the book of John and you will see many more specifics and actually very likely be quite surprised. A basic internet search will be VERY elucidatory. If Christ died for our sins and his death was pre-ordained, how is it someone's fault? Ignorance occurs everywhere; however, when it is sponsored by carrying the God Flag, I can assure you God weeps.

Interestingly, a good friend of mine was a Theology major at a major American university studying with the Jesuits. The Jesuits are often considered the scholars of Christianity. Our current Pope is in fact the first Jesuit Pope. As I spoke with him about my troubles with the book of John he told me that the Jesuits spent the entire first semester criticizing and finding flaws in the book of John and had the students put it in its proper historical context. It was written many years after the synoptic gospels, Mathew, Mark and Luke and contains new miracles and stories never revealed in the first 3 books. Why? And why the anti-Semitic verses in this book never mentioned in the first 3 synoptic gospels? If you look at the history of the time, Christianity was a new religion trying to gain power. Around the time of the Counsel of Nicea, as scholars were trying to pick the proper gospels to represent the true life of Jesus, (and as you may or may not recall there were many to choose from), perhaps in the pursuit of the greater good, Machiavellian principles led them down a path with some unexpected consequences? Perhaps the ends did NOT justify the means?

In my opinion, why do churches spend so much time on everything BUT the master's words? The words written in red. How fabulous would church be if half of it was spent in discussion of what Christ's words meant to each individual? "Judge not lest you be judged". "He without sin cast the first stone". That's the church I want to attend. I want to discuss what the words written in red do to influence my life. Not what the other prophets did or said, or many of the didactic nuances, many of which are used to control, strengthen and enrich the church or used by the haters as justification for their ends. I apologize for sounding dogmatic, but growing up surrounded by antisemitism affects an individual greatly. Why does it exist so rampantly? I am certain Jesus would not approve. The Holocaust museum was as powerful as one can imagine. I suspect the whole purpose is to make sure we never forget. It can happen again.

Next we went to the Israel museum. It was very beautiful. I learned that Albert Einstein and subsequently Sigmund Freud were both asked to be the original prime minister of Israel. They wanted to found their country on science and technology and felt that either one of them would have been a wonderful start. In fact, Einstein's original theory of relatively is contained in the Israel museum. I was also moved by the Dead Sea scrolls and fascinated to learn more about the Essenes. I have been taught that they were an offshoot of the Egyptian mystery schools and possible even the source of Jesus the Christ.

During the day, while driving through the west bank, there was a fascinating discussion with my Palestinian Christian driver and my new guide. My previous Jewish guide would not enter into Bethlehem as it was Palestinian territory. The plight of the Palestinians is very sad. They are an educated, industrious, hardworking people. I have heard them called, ironically, the Jews of the Arab world. Nevertheless, their plight is a very difficult one with thousands of years of animosity and dissension with their Jewish neighbors. I said an earnest prayer on their behalf and I sincerely hope that they can someday have a homeland. The politics in Israel make the USA look simple.

Upon arrival in Bethlehem we came to the "manger". I have been taught in my teachings that Jesus was born in an Essene Grotto and nothing I witnessed that day dispelled that. In fact, I wonder how so many Christians can walk down into the CAVES in Bethlehem and think it was a manger? Oh well. Free thinking and religion are often counterintuitive statements.

There was very beautiful energy in the caves. I didn't get the overwhelming energy I felt in Galilee but it was a very special place and very spiritual. I did receive the full energy of the master while meditating in the cave where Jesus was laid after his birth. (See figure 18) Even more so then when touching the star signifying the spot of his birth. (See figures 19 and 20) The room was infused with the full effect of the force. God had clearly blessed this place.

The next day was my birthday, and as I wandered through a store in Bethlehem I was transfixed by a very special wood carving of the last supper. It was done by a famous Palestinian artist and the detail was exceptional and I was quite moved. My birthday present now sits on a shelf in my kitchen to this day. (See figure 21) Who knew? My Jewish home with a Baptist wife and a Palestinian sculpture of the last supper. God does have a sense of humor.

I ended my evening again at the western wall. My dove greeted me and I had a beautiful end to another glorious day in the Holy Lands. I would meditate every day there if I could but of course Capernaum would be a pretty amazing place to have daily meditations also.

LOVE

DAY 8

THIS DAY WAS my birthday so I was quite jovial and prepared for a new adventure. We started the day driving to Massada along the Dead Sea. It was 110 degrees. Some people will say "But it's the desert. Its dry heat". I'm from Florida. I say it was very hot. However, dry heat is different and very dangerous. One needs to make themselves hydrate continuously or you will get into serious trouble.

Massada was an old military fortress built on a high hill overlooking the dessert. It was an interesting morning and worth the visit, but no exceptional energy was found here.

We then went to Quaran to explore the sight where the Essenes lived and where the Dead Sea scrolls were found. (See figure 22) I was fascinated, again because of the history I was taught about the Essenes being a branch from the Egyptian Mystery Schools and possibly the source of Jesus. I found very good energy and it was a very unique place. Nevertheless, I was pretty sure I was not there before. No Déjà vu.

Finally, we went to the Mount of Olives overlooking the eastern side of the old city and the Arab world's holy golden domed mosque, (the dome of the rock) purportedly where Muhammed ascended into heaven and why it is still so sacred to the Muslim religion. (See figure 23) It was also where Jesus first overlooked Jerusalem according to the New Testament and got a donkey to ride through the old city. It was quite different energy as it was predominantly Arab, but very beautiful nonetheless.

Growing up raised as a Jew, I encountered significant prejudice. Some very overt, but often politely subterfuged but apparent if one listened to all the words being spoken. This was amongst Christians. I had always known the animosity between the Jews and the Arabs so I found it slightly uncomfortable, as silly as that may seem, to be surrounded by so many Arabs. The next day I was venturing into the Arab world with significant trepidation but the pyramids were my ultimate goal. Remember…have a plan.

I was growing my beard from the day I left Florida so I figured with my Semitic blood and a full beard, I might fit in more. How wrong I was. Everyone knew I was American.

I spent my birthday having a great dinner with my guide and a few drinks overlooking the old city on a rooftop. It was very beautiful. I had strangely no desire to go out and party. I had a lovely meditation and went to bed early. Tomorrow the Arab world.

LOVE

DAY 9: THE ARAB WORLD

As I SHOULD have expected, the day started crazy and I didn't understand why until months later. It was September 11th ironically enough, although the irony of the date eluded me until I began to write this book. The Twin Towers collapsed September 11, 2001, the morning after my 40th birthday party. We all knew what we were doing that day. September 11, 2015 was quite different, yet the same. My driver was to pick me up at a predetermined time and he was running late. I even had to call the parent company as I was concerned, as late for this company was 20 minutes early waiting for me. (It's why I called the Travel company fullprice.com. You get what you pay for). My driver called me back in 5 minutes and apologized and said he would be there in a few minutes as "he ran into some traffic". As we were leaving the city to drive towards the Jordan border crossing, we saw Palestinians running down the street in a mob like fashion. My Palestinian guide downplayed it and just said there was "some trouble at the dome of the rock". (The Golden Dome). In fact, this trouble was why he was late that morning. Little did I know that a year later, the troubles from that day were the genesis for the most recent Palestinian uprising in Jerusalem with all the associated killings and raids still going on since that day. Interestingly enough, my guide shared that he was significantly harassed the evening before with his wife at the grocery store they frequented regularly by the Israel authorities for the first time ever and "He would not be going back there". Synchronicity is everywhere.

Little did I know that the event that was playing out was very historically significant and was going to greatly compound my border crossing into Jordan. Sometime ignorance is bliss. I was cautioned by my guide beforehand and my driver again to just be patient and it would all work out. The heightened Israel/Palestinian tensions however, were the 800 pound gorilla in the room.

It was set up in advance for me to have "VIP" border crossing where everything was prearranged. What no one told me was I was going to pass 100 M16s or AK47s on both sides of the border with tensions cranked up on the anxiety meter. To make matters worse, I was there for about an hour and a half with my passport NOT in my possession. It was clearly time to say a prayer.

I rapidly realized that silence and being a good person with utmost respect was the order of the day. The ugly impatient American inside of me had to stay home. Whilst sitting in the lounge surrounded by Arabs dressed in mostly traditional garb, I felt more than a little uncomfortable. What enters one's mind at these times can be the craziest things in the world. I couldn't help but think of Marc Cohn's classic song "Walking in Memphis". Particularly the line where the bar maiden asked him, "Tell me are you a Christian child…"…. And he says, "Ma'am, I am tonight". This verse put a giant smile on my face and I knew all was going to be well. In fact, I decided my name if anyone asked (which they never did) in the Arab world was Scott Wilson (not Scott Wiesen). Like another former song says, "Whatever gets you through the night". Thank you Marc Cohn.

Interestingly though, when discussing the perceived dangers of the Middle East with Arabs and Israelis alike as an American, they just laughed. I heard on more than one occasion, that from what they read, America is much more dangerous! They read all the time how people in the USA are shooting each other constantly, blowing things up, mass machine gun murders in schools and malls, etc…. In fact, they imply that what they read about the dangers of America, make them feel a little better about where they live. Very fascinating food for thought for all of us.

The Arab crisis perhaps is one without a readily apparent solution. The Sunnis hate the Shiites and vice versa. They all hate the Jews and the Christians. What I wrote in my journal that evening was from a physician's description of an obscure disease without a cure, "The solution to this problem remains an enigma wrapped in a mystery".

The Dead Sea was amazingly beautiful. The Kempinski Ishtar resort was beyond plush. As I checked in, I was significantly upgraded to a private villa away from the main buildings right on the Dead Sea with a gorgeous gigantic balcony and stellar views. Just lucky I guess.

As I looked throughout my villa and saw one of the nicest over the top bathrooms complete with every possible amenity and a world famous spa to match (frequented by many celebrities and movie stars it turns out), I really missed my bride. She knew I needed to be alone on this journey. She would not impede my adventure at all. Nevertheless, this was her kind of place.

That evening I ate traditional Arab BBQ and watched Arab musicians play while a belly dancer also performed. It was quite lovely.

At bedtime, after my meditation, I wrote in my journal, "One God. One Love. May peace permeate everyone. Inshallah (God willing in Arabic...my favorite Arabic phrase).

LOVE

DAY 10

WHEN I PLANNED this trip, I knew the pyramids were my ultimate destination. Through some research I found the safest way to get there was through Jordan. I wanted a day or two in the middle of my journey to spiritually recharge and relax along the Dead Sea. At the time, I didn't know that there were no luxury resorts along the Israeli side of the Dead Sea as the land is like quicksand sinking into the earth. It is very dangerous. Hence, the luxury hotels were on the Jordanian side. A plan was progressing. Then again, like I said before, "Man plans, and God laughs".

This blessed day started with an amazing trip to the spa. I have traveled much of the world and although not the fan of spa's that my bride is, I have been to a few. This one could matchup to any in the world. There are none better I have ever encountered. I had a wonderful workout and shower and I was meditating awaiting my massage. I was deep, lost in the ether when they came to retrieve me. I was in a very special place we all like to be...complete serenity. During my massage, my spirit released completely and I was floating. It was then that I had my first inkling I was supposed to write a book. In fact at the time it came with a title..."Practicing medicine as a mystic". The plan began to get formulated.

Ironically, for the holidays, my older son Brett gave me a very beautiful diary. On the cover it said, "Thanks for being my Dad". Our relationship had been under continuous repair since divorcing his mother when he was 2 years old. We were always together but our relationship had been strained. Any divorced parent, especially fathers, know of what I am saying. For whatever reason, he had the foresight to give me the diary, and I used it as a journal during my journey. The notes from this journal were the basis for this book. That afternoon while in the infinity pool, I was surrounded by a wonderful group of Palestinians from Lebanon. They were discussing some medical issues with me, which is clearly never my first choice on vacation, but I answered their questions with patience and kindness and an open heart. Wow....was I rewarded.

They told me they were there as the guest of a Saudi Sheik. They took me down to the Dead Sea and we all shared a mud bath. Of course, since they were with the Royal Villa, we had private attendants to rinse us down and clean us. The healing properties of the Dead Sea are legendary and nothing I felt that day led me to feel any differently.

I left them, but they insisted I join them for a private party that evening at the Royal Villa to dine with the Sheik. As I discussed the potential evening with my wife, she had much trepidation understandably. There was concern over my Hebrew heritage and the fact that I knew none of these people. I promised to be careful and be home early, but I was going to attend. The problem was dinner was not scheduled till 10 pm. I had a beautiful mediation. I said a prayer, and off I went.

The Royal Villa was magnificent as expected. The Sheik had flown in his private chefs to prepare a 10 course feast with musicians and beautiful people around a very large table. It was an incredible experience and everyone went out of their way to make the experience as amazing as it could possibly be. My wife called twice as she was worried. I had promised to turn my phone on, which I never did on this journey. I told her I would leave by 2, but they would go till 5am. I didn't want to be rude as after all I was treated essentially as the guest of honor even by the Saudi Sheik who could not have been more gracious as were all his Arab guests.

Now I have stated clearly that every story in this book is 100% true but this next part still amazes me to this day. At 2am, a little drunk from delicious Johnny Walker Blue and a full belly, I said my goodbyes to my very gracious host and his friends. As I was leaving, they chanted in unison, including the Saudi Sheik, "USA. USA. USA." Three times of course. I was moved to tears. Something to ponder. Perhaps there is hope. Inshallah.

When I got home, I got this overwhelming urge to call a friend vacationing in Las Vegas to place $20 on 7 red on the Roulette wheel. Of course it hit the first try. Trust your instincts. It is the force telling you what to do. Open your eyes and your heart…God is great.

LOVE

LESSON 2 – SYNCHRONICITY

Pay attention to this one. Synchronicity is all around us and happens all the time. Usually most of us fail to pay attention. Wikipedia defines it as "the simultaneous occurrence of events that appear significantly related but have no discernable causal connection".

Well seekers...open your eyes and open your heart. Synchronicity is pervasive, we just usually ignore it. The "no discernable causal connection" is only not discernible to those unwilling to open their eyes and hearts. The causal connection is the force. It's God. If one pays attention, the whole world opens up to you. Synchronicity is all around us happening all the time. Look for it as you will be amazed how often you will recognize it once you start actually looking.

LOVE

DAY 11

My NEW GUIDE and driver arrived early the next morning. A little hungover, I arrived at Mount Nebo. This was as close as Moses ever got to the Holy Land. This was an incredible power spot sadly seen by very few Jews because of its location in Jordan. (See figures 24 and 25) Once again the holy spirt came to me and I felt all the blessings and power of the force come upon me. It was truly magnificent. My Muslim guide witnessed this and could sense my aura change from this drunk he picked up at the hotel to a spiritual being and our relationship changed completely at that point. He was also a very spiritual man. I sadly know very little about Islam, but as I stated before, many paths to the same truth. The fundamental truths such as love, pure heart, good intentions, the laws of karma, and the golden rule are present in any religious path to God. As I always expected, the difference is essentially mostly semantics. One God. One Love.

Once my guide opened up as he recognized my spirituality, the journey changed immensely. We had a wonderful discussion on the plight of the Palestinians and the troubles in the Arab world. More importantly, he also realized the differences were mostly superficial amongst all religions.

He took me to a place doing original Jordanian ceramic art work and I was moved to purchase a few lovely memorable pieces. (See figure 26) Beautiful naturally colored stone, cut and hand inlaid into beautiful ceramic plates and vases. We must always pay our good fortune forward. In my life, it has always been to contribute to the arts. Back home I have sponsored a group called Live Art for going on 15 years now. As a drummer, I had given up music from age 23-40 while furthering my medical career. When I started playing again is when we formed Live Art. It is essentially a warehouse where artists can come play music and make art with no financial obligations. Over the years, the place has garnered its own magical aura. We have even had a few Grammy award winning musicians that are amazed at the beautiful energy the place creates. The biggest honor I get to this day, and I have heard it more than once, is when an accomplished musician pulls me aside and says, "I haven't had this much fun playing music since I was very young". No strings attached art and music just for pure love. Pay it forward.

After we left the artists, we went to a church full of mosaics and traditional Jordanian hand inlaid colored stone. There was one Mosaic of Jesus after the crucifixion being laid on the slab I saw in Jerusalem. Once again, the Holy Spirit entered me and I had an amazing meditation there. A delicious traditional Arab lunch at a famous Jordanian restaurant followed with another enlightening conversation with my guide. Lunch was followed with a fabulous 2 ½ hour nap on the drive to Petra with a lazy night after that. (See figure 27) Petra tomorrow…then Egypt.

LOVE

DAY 12

Petra is truly one of the wonders of the world. (See figures 28 and 29) I was amazed at the fabulous carvings out of the mountain. It is breathtaking. It was an unexpected honor to visit there. I would encourage anyone to go visit as the relationship between Jordan and the USA will never be better than it is right now because of the Isis conflict and our countries symbiotic interests. Go.

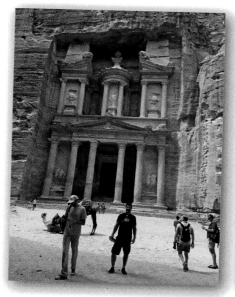

Interestingly, when I first was planning this trip, people told me I was crazy to go to the Middle East. "It is very unsafe". I am a 55 year old man.

It has NEVER been safe to travel to the Middle East since I have been alive. I encourage everyone to make the journey to the heart of the world and have their own life changing adventure. You can die anywhere. When we live in fear the enemy wins.

Whilst Petra was breathtakingly beautiful and architecturally miraculous, it was not necessarily a spiritual hotbed. Probably the most interesting moment I had was during one of my meditations in a cave. I was suddenly compelled to stop, which I never do. I had the feeling there was a scorpion around me although I have never seen one in my life and I was never warned of any here. I awoke and laughingly told my guide, who was Muslim (so he definitely understood prayer as they do it 5 times a day and loved that I did it regularly) about my current meditation and he was astounded when I mentioned the scorpion. He told me he had just felt the same thing and had killed one while I was meditating! Synchronicity. Pay attention.

Petra was an amazing part of the journey and I knew the precious present was everything. Nevertheless, I knew I was finally heading to Egypt tomorrow and the pyramids and this had always been my ultimate destination. I knew I needed to figure out a way to get into the great chamber and meditate. I had no idea what awaited me but I was truly ready.

We drove back to Amman, Jordan for a 6a.m. flight to Cairo in the am. Surprisingly, in the Four Seasons in Amman, I had one of the greatest Thai meals of my life as there was a visiting famous chef from Thailand there for a few weeks. I am always happy to be surprised and ready to be lucky. Remember, "Luck favors the prepared mind".

Up to then, it had already been the journey of a lifetime. It was an amazing growth period for me. My ability to connect with the force was almost synchronous with my asking. Remember the words written in red. "Ask and it shall be given. Seek and ye shall find. Knock and it shall be opened unto you". As importantly, if you dare to do, you will be given the power to do. Tomorrow Egypt.

LOVE

DAY 13

As I ARRIVED in Egypt, flying over Cairo, I was amazed at how large and how many millions of people there seemed to be. Conception and reality are not always the same. It reminds me of the difference between actuality and reality. Actuality is the divine truth; reality is something we create on our own. We all live in different realities. Did you ever wonder how 2 people can be at the same place at the same time yet there description of the event, the surroundings, and the people there are completely different? Everyone lives in their own reality.

As I disembarked in Cairo airport, I was personally met and whisked through customs within 5 minutes with my bag in hand. Sometimes traveling with Fullprice.com is wonderful. I anticipated a lengthy discussion with immigration having come from Israel recently as Israeli's were specifically told not to travel to Egypt at that time. Let me just say it now. I did NOT feel safe in Egypt at all. Cairo was the scariest most dangerous city I have ever seen. The driving was truly insane also as there were essentially no rules at all. I felt very fortunate to have my 6 foot 4 inch Egyptologist ex-military guide (presumably armed) at my side the entire time. This country felt to be on the precipice of disaster at any moment. I am an eternal optimist but I never left my hotel once alone the 2 days I was there. My Egyptian guide was wonderful. I had just finished my journal entry from the day before on the short flight over and within 5 minutes of us meeting, my guide quoted my last journal entry from day twelve. "Ask and it shall be given. Seek and ye shall find. Knock and the door shall be open unto you". I showed him my journal and we both recognized synchronicity was in place. My guide and I subsequently entered into an esoteric mystical conversation. We had a wonderful connection. I shared with him a few of my stories of my adventure so far including my white dove. He told me some of the trials and tribulations he encountered as a Muslim and an Egyptologist and a light seeker himself. It was going to be a special visit to Egypt....Inshallah.

Our first stop was the Egyptian museum. As an avid student of history, I was very excited to see the world famous Egyptian museum. They were actually building a new museum elsewhere as the current one was very old. Then again, so were the contents. The history was amazing. As we walked around, we got to one particular Egyptian burial casket (one of many). For whatever reason I KNEW immediately who it was. It was Amenhotep IV also known as Akneton, before my guide told me. I saw the cover of his tomb and felt this incredible energy. I had told my guide about my interest in him on the drive there. To his credit, he was not surprised at all that I knew. Amenhotep IV is credited by many as creating the world's first monotheistic religion which went against the prevailing polytheistic Egyptian beliefs. Sadly, but historically very importantly, as the reigning priests had all the money and power, they arranged to have him killed. Change was not in their interests. More death and violence whilst carrying the God flag. So sad.

The Egyptian museum is a must see visit if one has the courage to go to Egypt. I didn't like all the glorification of the polytheism of Egyptian worship, but I must confess I was very drawn to Osiris. I felt drawn to his energy. My guide just laughed and wouldn't tell me more about it until later. I had my best meditation of the day by the mummy of Amenhotep IV and once again had an infusion of the Holy Spirit. He was a very blessed man, sadly forgotten by much of history and the world.

The day had started very early for my 6 am flight and I was very tired. My guide had arranged a private tour through 2 of Cairo's most famous mosques. For a multitude of reasons, I asked to skip them. My guide, which I had developed a rapport and respect with in our short time together, beseeched me to go visit the mosques. I of course conceded, and I was very glad I went. He was a devout Muslim and we had a wonderful talk about Islam in both mosques. We sat quietly on a rug in prayer and then had a very enlightening conversation about the plight of Islam and the Muslim people intertwining and coexisting with the rest of the world. As always, a problem with no discrete answer. "An Enigma wrapped in a mystery".

We waited and conversed until it was time for the call to prayer. A very gifted singer arrived in non-traditional dress which was somewhat surprising to me. He sang the call to prayer broadcast out to the streets of Cairo. WOW! Hollywood with all its magic had nothing on the power instantly created by the amazing vibrations this singer created. I would highly recommend this experience to any seeker of the light as it was very moving with great energy and infusion of the Holy Spirit. Many paths to the same truth.

I promised my guide I would someday read the Koran. Isn't it strange that part of me was afraid to even download it to my IPad for fear of the government then watching me? To quote the great Benjamin Franklin, "Those who can give up essential liberty to obtain a little temporary safety deserve neither". (I downloaded the Koran the day I wrote this).

We then traveled back and I was dropped off at the Four Seasons Cairo. I had a lovely room overlooking the Nile River and the sunset was amazing. Synchronicity was in place again as of course it was also the night of the Islamic crescent moon at sunset. I took a picture with a rose from my room and the sunset over the Nile which is a very special photo for me to this day. (See figure 30) I had a simple dinner and spent the evening reading about the great pyramid and preparing for my initiation tomorrow in the great chamber. I shaved for the first time in a couple of weeks and I had a fabulous meditation in preparation. I had absolutely no idea what awaited me tomorrow but I was as prepared as I ever was going to be. Inshallah.

LOVE

Day 14 the Pyramids

As I awoke that morning, I was filled with excitement but I wanted to temper my enthusiasm and most of all I wanted to have no expectations. I had no idea what awaited me inside the great pyramid but it had taken me 54 years to get here and I wanted to enjoy it all. In high school there was a group of three of us that were all likeminded seekers. We made the vows of youth to all meet at the great pyramid for the millennium. Well as the great John Lennon once said, "Life is what happens when you are busy making other plans." We never made it …..Then.

My wonderful Egyptologist spiritual guide had arranged for me to be first in line with a special pass to go into the great chamber. I spoke at the beginning of this diatribe about my difficultly climbing. For whatever reason, I knew that I would be fine today. Yoda was again on my side. "Do or do not. There is no try."

As I arrived in the inner chamber I was very tired as I practically ran all the way up so I could be first. The heart of a child, but with the same stupid results that children are often left with. I was very winded. Subsequently, it took me a few minutes to get into that special place inside my heart. Once I did the energy was amazing. As people came and went, the energy changed but I had about a 20 minutes span where it was just myself and another seeker. Twice I felt myself lifting out of my body but never completely. It was very special. The immense power and energy created by the world's largest energy source was awe-inspiring. My body was vibrating continuously at such a high rate it was like nothing I have ever experienced. I said my prayers and rode the amazing energy wave until I was filled to the brim. About an hour in, the

Egyptian pyramid security came and told myself and the other seeker there that it was time for us to leave. No problem. We followed him out.

As we walked down the pyramid I got another very special treat. We got a rare glimpse into the queen's chamber as he unlocked it for us and gave us a few moments of private time. It was very special, but brief. My guide said all these years; he has never known anyone able to enter the queen's chamber like that. Another gift from God. The New Testament spends time on the birth of Jesus and a few pages when he was 13 going to Jerusalem for the first time and then he starts his beautiful ministry at age 30. There are books available however that discuss Jesus's early years and some say his final initiation and attainment of the Christhood came in the great chamber just before he started his ministry? Nothing I saw or felt today changed that belief for me. One of the most immense energy spots on planet earth.

As I exited, I was completely pleased with my experience as I had no prior expectations. My guide sat me in our air conditioned van and gave me an extensive history of the building of the pyramid, its magnetic placement, and its geography. My guide reminded me of my fascination with Osiris at the Egyptian museum previously. The Egyptian God was named for the constellation Orion. Always one of my favorite landmarks in the sky. The three pyramids relative size and placement is identical to the constellation Orion, deliberately. It was why he had laughed the day before. More synchronicity. There are many fabulous facts about the great pyramids. I encourage any and all of you to spend a few hours reading about some of these amazing statistics and stories.

My guide then encouraged me to exit the van and spend a few moments admiring the pyramids. It was then I SAW IT! My spirit guide was back from the western wall. My white dove. I couldn't believe it. I was humbled beyond belief. I got my guide out of the van to show him as I had previously told him the story. He thought I was crazy because he couldn't see it. He said, "We're in the middle of the desert (not really anymore) there are no doves!" I took a photo and enlarged it and showed him the dove up close and of course he was blown away. The dove was in the center of the pyramid. (See figures 31 and 32) Once again, I was moved to tears and cried like a baby. My white dove had followed me the whole journey. I had dreamed a few nights before that he would be at the pyramids but certainly never thought it consciously. I knew then my journey was complete and I found whatever it is that I was looking for. Wow! God is great.

One of my favorite sayings I tell people all the time is "Be careful what you ask for as you just may get it." Wish fulfillment is a tricky thing because we are only human and we don't always know what we really want. Like Mick Jagger said, "You can't always get what you want, but if you try sometimes you just might find, you get what you need".

After reestablishing some decorum, we continued on to the sphynx. (See figures 33 and 34) My final infusion of the Holy Spirit occurred in the temple below the sphynx. My guide was smiling and showed me a power spot in the corner of the temple and asked me to go there and pray. It was infused with an energy that somehow he knew of? As I stood there and closed my eyes and meditated, I was filled with the full power of the force. I saw an enlarging red orb around the area of my third eye. It slowly transformed into on ankh. The Egyptian symbol of fertility. Of course, I then bought one for my wife and daughter with a red stone in the middle. It was a very odd sensation, made even more so as my guide knew it to be a power spot.

As we ate lunch at a spot overlooking the pyramids, my white dove sat outside. Of course. What I thought was a final farewell.

That evening as I wrote in my journal I realized how much I loved this journey and how important it was for me. It had been more than I ever could have hoped for and evolved even beyond my expectations. I wrote in my journal the following phrases....

1. Thank you God for all you have given me.
2. Love the Lord God with all your heart above all others.
3. Love your neighbor as you would yourself, although I prefer the golden rule. Do unto others as you would have others do onto you.

LOVE

DAY 15

I KNEW THIS was going to be a long travel day so I prepared myself to relax. Shockingly, Israel is still around because they have one of the best intelligence services in the world. Arriving in immigration back in Tel Aviv, I expected a long arduous interview as I had just spent a week in the Arab world. I was questioned for 30 minutes in New York because of my itinerary before even being given a boarding pass! However, on arrival, never filling out any forms, the immigration agent looked at her computer and said, "I hope you had a wonderful journey Dr. Wiesen" and I was on my way. Silly me. They likely knew everything I did and where I went my entire journey. Hence they still exist surrounded by people who want to blow them up every day. I felt much safer in Israel. Quite interesting actually. My flight out wasn't until about 7 that evening so I got a day room at the first hotel I stayed at. It turned out God wasn't quite done with me yet. My final connection occurred while sitting in the pool relaxing thinking about my adventure (absent any bachelorette parties). I saw some white seagulls flying over the Mediterranean Sea and all I could think of was my white dove….It was then my white dove literally flew right in front of me across the pool watching me the whole time. It was almost in slow motion. God is great. USA…. I'm coming home.

LOVE

PROLOGUE

ALMOST A YEAR later, as I sit overlooking the Atlantic Ocean and recollecting my adventure, I realized a prologue was in order. I am just an ordinary man. I am like most seekers reading this book. The main difference is I had the courage to go on my vision quest and have an adventure. I opened my eyes, ears, and my heart and was prepared to accept whatever awaited me. The blessings will stay with me forever.

I remember writing an email to my adopted father in Kennedy Airport awaiting my flight home to Florida. He has helped me over the years to guide me along my spiritual path. He wrote back some of the greatest wisdom and exactly what I needed to hear at that point and time. He said, "Be careful of the reentry when you come back to reality".

As I stated, towards the end of my journey I could call upon the source almost at will and it came to me often. It was a magnificent experience I will never forget. Sadly, it is not the everyday reality for most of us including myself.

I retrospectively became aware of the benefits of not having a cell phone interrupting all your thoughts, a surgery schedule, problem patients, fighting children, a bride that requires my love and attention, friends and family that require time and love, etc.... It became obvious to me at that point and time that part of the reason I was able to vibrate at such a high level for so long had to do with my ability to separate from the mundane world and during my journey live solely in the spiritual world.

Although my life is clearly blessed and I am very thankful for the multitude of gifts I have been given for my life in the mundane world...it is still that. (By mundane world, it is meant to imply life on the physical earthly plane). Perhaps this finally helped me more fully understand why the rose exists in the center of the cross. Our own self, the rose, at the crossroads of where life meets itself in both the mundane and the spiritual world. The Rose Cross.

Over this last year, having indeed crash landed on reentry, as I was warned, I have been trying to incorporate one of the most difficult things for a spiritual seeker. The balance between life in the mundane world and life in the spiritual world. Finding happiness in the mundane world is one of the great secrets of life, and much harder than most of us realize.

So did this "Physician Heal Thyself"? Healing and wellness is the never ending journey of our physical and spiritual being. This adventure helped fill my heart with love and my body with the spiritual nutrition it craved to continue to grow. I am prepared to finish the back nine of life with renewed vigor and the "knowing" that comes with communing with the source.

Good luck on your own journeys and adventures. I hope this book has inspired you to do that very thing. Try to find the balance between the mundane world and your mystical pursuit. Find your rose in your own cross. God is always there to light your path.

LOVE

ABOUT THE AUTHOR

S COTT WIESEN IS a practicing gastroenterologist in Naples, Florida. He is happily married with four beautiful children. In his spare time, he is an avid musician, sailor, amateur chef, soccer coach, and dad. His pursuit of the mystical truth is a never ending journey with a strong desire to spread light to all those willing to accept it. He is currently planning his next bucket list trip to Tibet. For now, Scott plans to continue to relish every moment of the precious present. He understands that the only way to learn how to write is to just DO IT! The author relishes the opportunity to master the skills with time, to communicate his thoughts more effectively and illuminatingly. Please come... let's take this journey together.

LOVE